LITTLE BOOK OF

LITTLE BOOK OF

First published in the UK in 2014

© Demand Media Limited 2014

www.demand-media.co.uk

Printed and bound in Europe

ISBN 978-1-910270-58-5

Contents

Introduction

It is not unusual to walk down the street and see a variety of people with tattoos; however it is not a modern practise...

Tattooing has been practised throughout the world for thousands of years. There is evidence of extant tattooing on the preserved skin of a South American Chincorros mummy which dates back to 6000 BC!

In recent times tattoos have become more popular and socially accepted in many parts of the world. This has led to an increase in new tattoo artists, many of whom have fine arts training. There have also been advancements in tattoo pigments and tattoo technology which means there has been a significant improvement in the quality of tattoos.

Tattoos are viewed by different ancient and modern cultures very differently. Some of these views are detailed in the following sections:

CHINA

The Ancient Chinese considered tattoos a barbaric practise. Even up until the Qing Dynasty (1644 – 1912), it was common to tattoo characters, such as 囚 (prisoner) to convicted criminals faces. Although it was rare, slaves were sometimes tattooed to display ownership.

PHILLIPINES

Tattoos have been a part of Filipino life since the pre-Hispanic colonization of the Philippine Islands in the 1500's. Some believed that tattoos had magical qualities, but to others they were a form of rank and accomplishments. They were first documented by the European Spanish explorers in the late 1700's, but long before European exploration tattooing was a widespread tradition among the islands.

EUROPE

10th century Arab traveller Ahmad ibn Fadlan wrote that when he encountered the Scandinavian Rus' tribe in the early 10th century, they were tattooed "from fingernails to neck" with dark blue "tree patterns" and other "figures". Tattoos were considered remaining elements of paganism and were generally legally prohibited during the gradual process of Christianization in Europe (7th – 15th centuries).

NEW ZEALAND

The indigenous Māori people of New Zealand practised a form of tattooing called ta moko which involves carving the skin with chisels rather than puncturing with needles which leaves the skin with groves as opposed to a smooth service.

In pre European Māori culture, most high ranking people received moko; those that didn't receive moko were considered a lower social status. Tā moko signalled status and rank, in traditional times it was to make a person more attractive to the opposite sex. Tā moko was also considered an important milestone in between childhood & adulthood and was occurred alongside many rites & rituals.

TAIWAN

Facial tattoos of the Taiwanese tribe Atayal tribe are called ptasan. Only those with tattoos could marry and after death only those with tattoos could cross the sprit bridge to the afterlife.

In order to earn his facial tattoo's a man would have to bring back at least one human head to demonstrate he can protect his homeland and a woman would have to master the skill of weaving to demonstrate her coming of age and maturity.

SAMOA

Like other Polynesian cultures, Samoans have significant and unique tattoos; they have two gender specific and culturally significant tattoos. Male tattoos are called pe'a and cover area from the knees up towards the ribs; their tattoos are intricate and geometrical designs. Female tattoos are called malu which are usually lighter designs than the pe'a and cover the area from just below the knee to the upper thigh.

In Samoan society the pe'a and malu are viewed with cultural pride and identity, they are also a hallmark of manhood and womanhood. There is much societal significance in Samoan tattoos; males with a pe'a are known as soga'imiti and they are respected for their courage.

Those who are not tattooed are generally known as telefua or telenoa meaning naked. If men begin, but do not complete, the tattooing ordeal (mainly due to pain or rarely due to the inability to pay the tattooist adequately) they are called pe'a mutu, a mark of shame. These tattoos take many weeks to complete and the art of applying them by hand is a tradition that has been unbroken for thousands of years and is often passed from father to son. Tools and techniques have changed little over time.

GREAT BRITAIN

Captain James Cook made three voyages to the South Pacific between 1766 & 1779; it was on his 1769 expedition to Tahiti that he first noted down observations of the indigenous people having tattoos. His Expedition Botanist & Science Officer, Sir Joseph Banks, along with many more of his men came back with tattoos as did ordinary men and sailors which led to the association between sailors and tattoos. In the 19th century tattoos were associated with sailors, the lower class and criminals. By the late 19th century it became fashionable among the upper classes, including royalty although it was largely rejected by the middle class. Tattoos have become more socially acceptable and fashionable, although they are less prominent on figures of authority.

According to the American Academy of Dermatology, there are five different types of tattoo; traumatic, or natural, tattoos, amateur & professional tattoos, identification tattoos, cosmetic tattoos & medical tattoos. We will look at these five different types of tattoos or below.

TRAUMATIC TATTOOS

Traumatic tattoos are tattoos that result from injury, for example asphalt from a road injury. Coal miners developed these characteristic tattoos when coal dust got into wounds, this can also occur with gunpowder. Whether deliberate or accidental, stabbing using a pencil and pen can give these tattoos as graphite or ink gets left beneath the skin.

AMATEUR & PROFESSIONAL TATTOOS
The symbolism and impact of tattoos varies in different cultures and in different places. They serve as rites of passage, marks of status & rank, punishment, talismans, protection, religious & spiritual devotion and as the marks of outcasts, slaves and convicts. Today people choose to be tattooed for artistic, sentimental/memorial and religious reasons among others. Tattoos can also symbolise their belonging or identification with particular groups, including criminal groups.

IDENTIFICATION TATTOOS
The most well known example of forcibly tattooing people for identification purposes is in the Nazi concentration camps during the Holocaust. This practise was introduced in Auschwitz in 1941 to identify the bodies of registered prisoners in the concentration camps.

As early as the Zhou dynasty (1046 – 256 BC), Chinese authorities would use facial tattoos as a punishment for certain crimes or to mark prisoners & slaves. The Roman Empire also employed this practise for gladiators & slaves. By law Roman soldiers were required to have identifying tattoos to make desertion difficult.

Tattoos are sometimes used by forensic pathologists to help them identify burned, putrefied or mutilated bodies.

COSMETIC TATTOOS
When used as a form of cosmetics, tattooing includes permanent make up and hiding or neutralizing skins discolorations. A growing trend in the US and UK is to place artistic tattoos over the surgical scars of a mastectomy.

MEDICAL TATTOOS
Medical tattoos are used to ensure instruments are properly located for repeated application of radiotherapy and are also used in some forms of breast reconstruction. Tattooing can also be used to convey medical information about the wearer (blood group, a medical condition etc).

Members of the Waffen-SS in Nazi German had tattoos to identify the individuals' blood type. When the war ended, these were taken to be almost perfect evidence of being the Waffen-SS leading to potential arrest & prosecution. This led to a number of ex-Waffen-SS to shoot themselves in the arm with a gun removing the tattoo.

Jaysin

Burgess

JAYSIN BURGESS BIOGRAPGHY

Born and bred in Chicago, Illinois my interest in tattoos started at a fairly early age...

My father was a marine and had a big eagle wrapping around an American flag with USMC below and from the earliest of memories I wondered how it got there. My Uncle was a biker and was covered in them including a very badly done portrait of Charles Manson on his belly as I recall. All through school I was never very good at any subjects except art.

My very first tattoo was on my best friend Andrew, it was done using a needle, thread & India Ink. He had a few of my early tattoos, even when I progressed to rigging up hair clippers, poor fool! (this is not recommended in any way!).

He is now at rest but thanks to him my career had begun. I spent quite a few years tattooing for fun out the house not seeing the potential I had. After I found out my third daughter was on her way I decided I needed to make a move quick and start doing something I loved for her benefit. I started tattooing every spare hour I had and drawing when I wasn't tattooing.

I started working in a street shop shortly before her birth, the money was great but the tattooing was very restrictive and unimaginative. That lasted about 3 weeks then I went to see a friend at another shop that was a custom shop more along the lines I was looking to work at. It lasted about a year and the shop went down the drain due to poor management to say the least.

Following the news I went around to all the decent shops in Newcastle upon Tyne and was about to give up and I found out about an opening at Northside Tattooz with Allan Lowther, a shop I only dreamed of being able to work for a great reputation filled with amazing artists. I have never looked back and am continually growing and pushing to be better.

I don't want anyone to think it was an easy road and wish I went through the traditional method of getting an apprenticeship as I would have been miles farther than I am at the minute. It was a fight and still is every day. I paint, draw and tattoo continually and I am always thinking of what's next.

Work hard and play little, it's the only way.

10 TATTOOS BY **JAYSIN BURGESS**

TATTOOS BY **JAYSIN BURGESS**

TATTOOS BY **JAYSIN BURGESS**

TATTOOS BY **JAYSIN BURGESS**   **15**

TATTOOS BY **JAYSIN BURGESS**

18

TATTOOS BY **JAYSIN BURGESS**

TATTOOS BY **JAYSIN BURGESS**

TATTOOS BY **JAYSIN BURGESS**

TATTOOS BY **JAYSIN BURGESS**

TATTOOS BY **JAYSIN BURGESS**

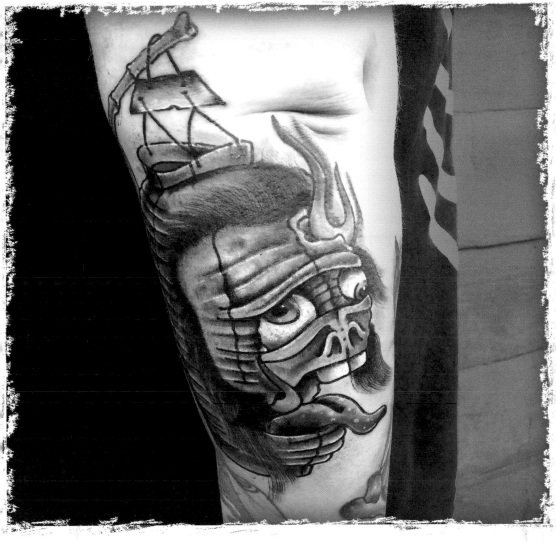

TATTOOS BY **JAYSIN BURGESS**

TATTOOS BY **JAYSIN BURGESS**

TATTOOS BY **JAYSIN BURGESS** 33

TATTOOS BY **JAYSIN BURGESS**

TATTOOS BY **JAYSIN BURGESS**

TATTOOS BY **JAYSIN BURGESS**

TATTOOS BY **JAYSIN BURGESS**

TATTOOS BY **JAYSIN BURGESS**

TATTOOS BY **JAYSIN BURGESS**

TATTOOS BY **JAYSIN BURGESS**   **43**

TATTOOS BY **JAYSIN BURGESS**

TATTOOS BY **JAYSIN BURGESS**

TATTOOS BY **JAYSIN BURGESS**

TATTOOS BY **JAYSIN BURGESS**   47

TATTOOS BY **JAYSIN BURGESS**

TATTOOS BY **JAYSIN BURGESS**

52　　TATTOOS BY **JAYSIN BURGESS**

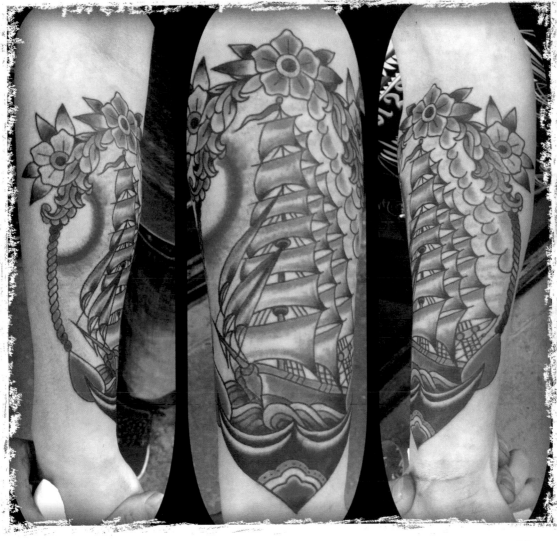

TATTOOS BY **JAYSIN BURGESS**   **53**

TATTOOS BY **JAYSIN BURGESS**

TATTOOS BY **JAYSIN BURGESS**

TATTOOS BY **JAYSIN BURGESS**

TATTOOS BY **JAYSIN BURGESS**

TATTOOS BY **JAYSIN BURGESS**

TATTOOS BY **JAYSIN BURGESS** 61

TATTOOS BY **JAYSIN BURGESS**

TATTOOS BY **JAYSIN BURGESS**

TATTOOS BY **JAYSIN BURGESS**

TATTOOS BY **JAYSIN BURGESS**

TATTOOS BY **JAYSIN BURGESS**

Rob Fielder

My name is Rob Fielder and I work at Northside Tattooz in Newcastle-upon-Tyne...

I started out drawing tattoo designs in school and spent a lot of my spare time drawing. I became interested in tattooing watching my dad get tattooed from a very early age and have been around the industry a lot of my life because of that. From the age of 16 I started to attend tattoo conventions and became more and more interested seeing how it was done and became totally in love with the art form.

I managed to get into a shop in Dorking, Surrey called Eternal Tattoos as a body piercer at the age of 19 after years of trying to get an apprenticeship, working for Ruth and Robb, alongside their other artist Stevie, but unfortunately after 2 years I could not afford the travel to get there and found myself having to leave. As I thought it was all doom and gloom Dale at Tattooland U.K. in Woking, Surrey, took me on again as their resident piercer and after a few months I became his tattoo apprentice.

I was so happy I was finally there but I still had a long way to go! I spent the next year and a half working as hard as I could; mopping floors, cleaning grips, running errands, drawing, all whilst still piercing. After this time Dale let me do my first tattoo on one of my good friends after a few practises. I then did several tattoos for free before I became confident enough and capable enough to start tattooing properly. I stayed there for about a year then moved to Newcastle-upon-Tyne to continue in my adventure! I started working at Arther T Sharpes before moving to another studio and ending up where I am now. I work alongside Allan Lowther and many other talented artists. I've since done several tattoo conventions myself including Brighton and Frankfurt. My favourite styles to work in are classic traditional and japanese although I am capable of most styles that I learned in my apprenticeship.

TATTOOS BY **ROB FIELDER**

TATTOOS BY **ROB FIELDER**

TATTOOS BY **ROB FIELDER**

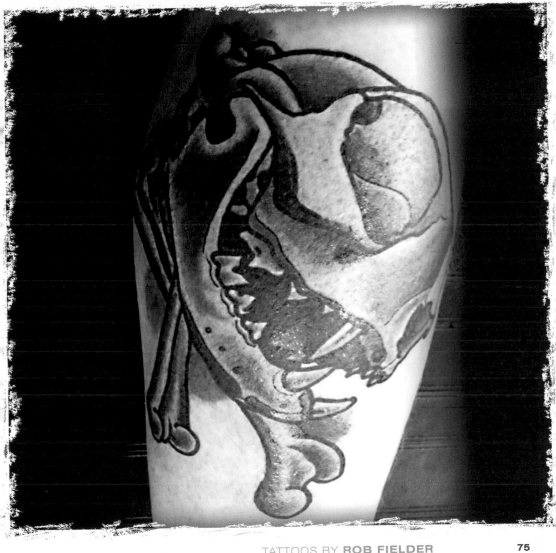

TATTOOS BY **ROB FIELDER**

TATTOOS BY **ROB FIELDER**

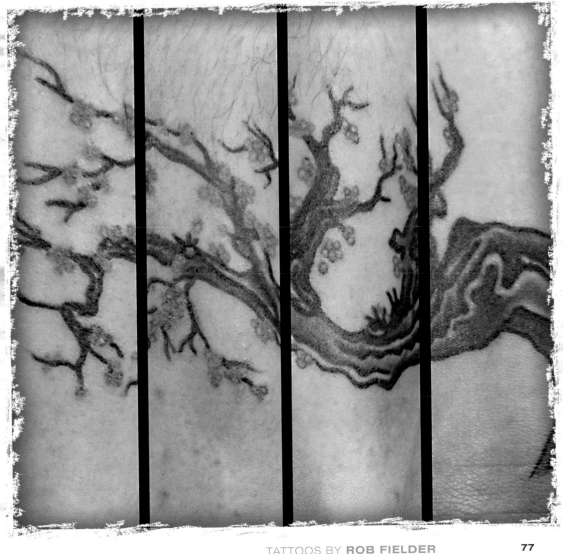

TATTOOS BY **ROB FIELDER**

TATTOOS BY **ROB FIELDER**

TATTOOS BY **ROB FIELDER**

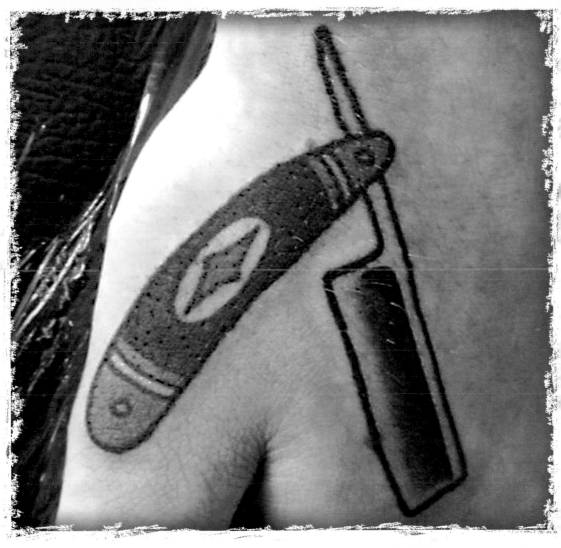

TATTOOS BY **ROB FIELDER**

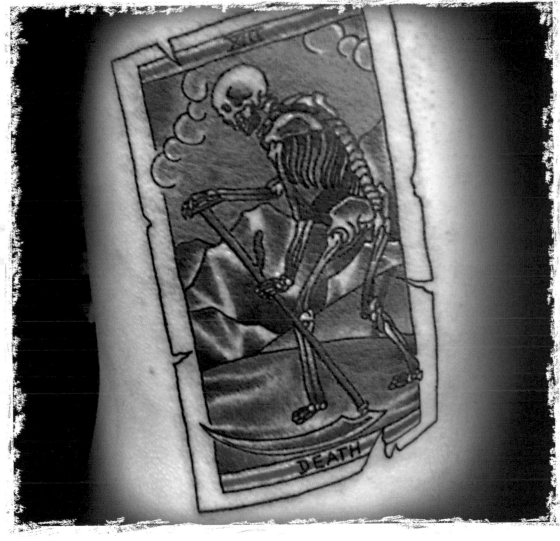

XIII

DEATH

TATTOOS BY **ROB FIELDER**

TATTOOS BY **ROB FIELDER**

TATTOOS BY **ROB FIELDER**

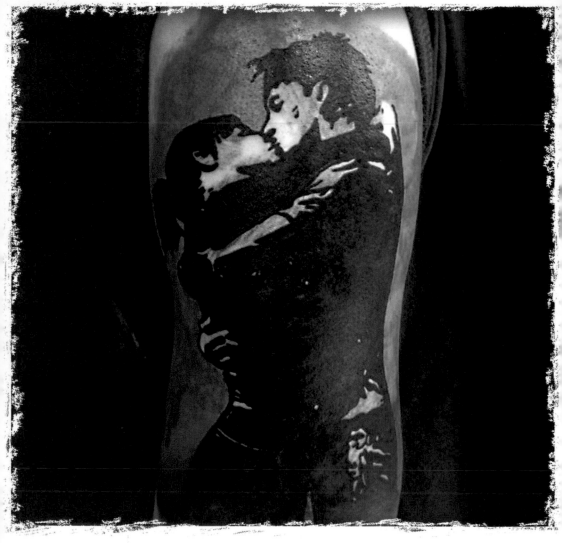

TATTOOS BY **ROB FIELDER**

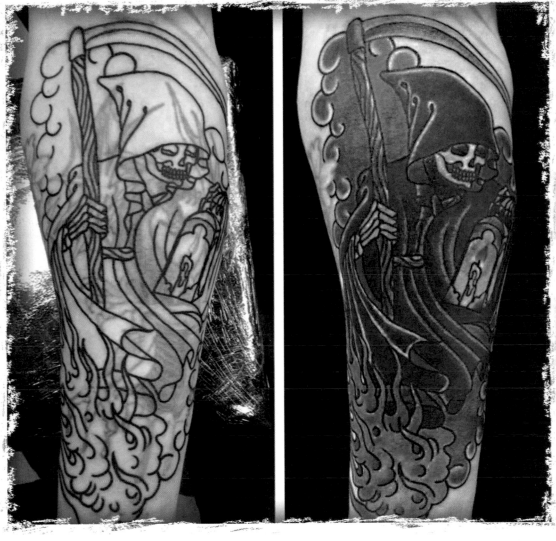

TATTOOS BY **ROB FIELDER**

TATTOOS BY **ROB FIELDER**

94	TATTOOS BY **ROB FIELDER**

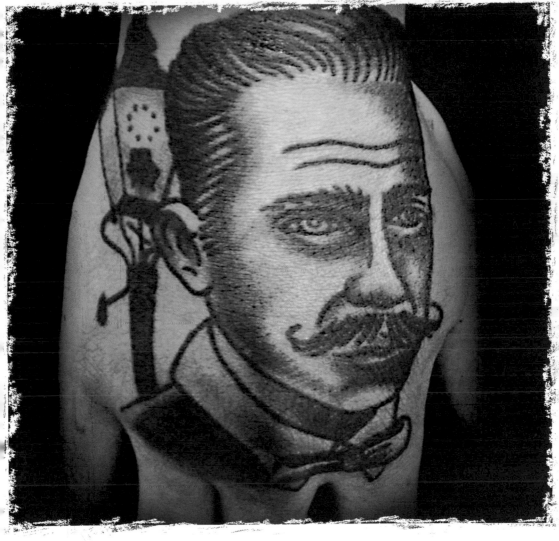

TATTOOS BY **ROB FIELDER**

TATTOOS BY **ROB FIELDER**

TATTOOS BY **ROB FIELDER**

TATTOOS BY **ROB FIELDER**

TATTOOS BY **ROB FIELDER**

TATTOOS BY **ROB FIELDER**

TATTOOS BY **ROB FIELDER**

TATTOOS BY **ROB FIELDER**

TATTOOS BY **ROB FIELDER**

TATTOOS BY **ROB FIELDER**

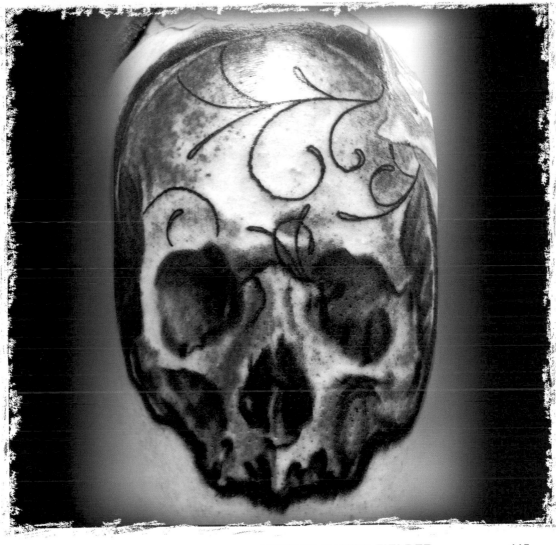

TATTOOS BY **ROB FIELDER**

TATTOOS BY **ROB FIELDER**

TATTOOS BY **ROB FIELDER**

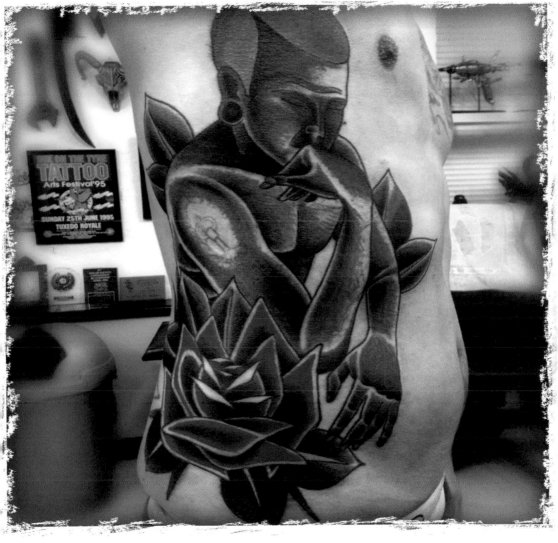

TATTOOS BY **ROB FIELDER**

TATTOOS BY **ROB FIELDER**

TATTOOS BY **ROB FIELDER**

TATTOOS BY **ROB FIELDER**   **127**

Design & Artwork: ALEX YOUNG

Published by: DEMAND MEDIA LIMITED

Publisher: JASON FENWICK

Introduction & Research: DAISY RAINSBOROUGH